AF255217

SONGS OF THE BELOVED

SONGS

OF

THE

BELOVED

Life, Love, and Learning

S. J. BEGUELY

RESOURCE *Publications* · Eugene, Oregon

SONGS OF THE BELOVED
Life, Love, and Learning

Resource Publications
An Imprint of Wipf and Stock Publishers
199 W. 8th Ave., Suite 3
Eugene, OR 97401

www.wipfandstock.com

PAPERBACK ISBN: 978-1-6667-8430-5
HARDCOVER ISBN: 978-1-6667-8431-2
EBOOK ISBN: 978-1-6667-8432-9
VERSION NUMBER 08/18/23

This book is dedicated to my wife, Sue. Many of the poems were written for her, so she has been an inspiration in that sense, but she has also inspired me with her own determination, persistence and courage in the face of adversity. Together we are fulfilling our life purpose, and together we will go on to achieve even more through the wonderful God we serve.

Prophesy to these bones
      Dry bones,
hear the word of the Lord.
I will make breath enter you
and you will come to Life,

        thus says the Lord.

Good words are not just bones, they come to life,
give healing, and peace for our assurance.
May these good bones in every true heart thrive
by the Spirit filled with love,
in every circumstance.

Contents

LAST DAYS

THE WORLD, NATURE, AND LIFE

WORDLESS POEMS

Acknowledgements

I would like to thank all the people, family, friends and high school teaching colleagues, whose lives and words provided the inspiration for so many of these poems. My peers and teachers at Bible college also challenged my presuppositions and inspired much of my thought about tradition and the church, about the ineffable nature of God and my relationship to him. I am, of course, completely indebted to the Holy Spirit for his gentle, and sometimes insistent nudges, to take up the pen and express the things we all need to periodically take stock of, for this life and the next.

Devotion

THE FISHER KING

Hooked through the heart
drawn up to the light
step by step, a progress to execution
the death of flesh, working out salvation
when will he land me, the fisher king?

Barbs in my arms, cruel spikes in my legs
my stomach and lungs pierced, choking dregs
hooked also from below by lines of luciferian light
mundane cares steel points so piercing bright
can he land me, the fisher king?

I would rend my flesh, tear out them all
but what would remain, they pierce my soul?
The ichthus master plays his catch with care
here snapped a broken weaker line,
a gently prised out point right there,
how does he land me, the fisher king?

And though I struggle for him, yet I deviate
each rusted point that I withdraw, three deeper penetrate.
So, play me free great fisherman of men
their lines below will break, their blackened steel will bend
your strong line will land me, my fisher king.

As from the deepening jaws he draws me to the light
the hook straight through my heart becomes my sole respite
as weaker lines that coil and bind snap freely
and hooks of fisher demons melt away
you land me on your farthest shore, my fisher king.

Yet, mystery of all, his hook stays caught
to my delight and his, the line stays taut.

Eternity in my heart is his refrain
the love of Jesus nothing ever will restrain
you draw me in forever, my great fisher king.

Resurrection Sunday, March 30, 1997.

BROKEN GROUND, HOLY GROUND

Unless the Lord had given me help
I would soon have dwelt in the silence of death.
When I said, "My foot is slipping,"
your unfailing love, O Lord, supported me.

—Ps 94:17–18

Once I wandered, weeping, onto broken ground
stumbling aimlessly from love's sight and sound.
There I sowed my bitter seeds of hate,
drawing ever near to hell's high gate

Poisoned by the barbs of your indifference
(or so it seemed)
I wandered on a byroad past the fence.
That road led to a high road, that wide road
that leads to hell's black gate

Centered in my pain and loss, not yours
I fell sickly into the desponding moor.
So I wallowed, covered in slime and shite
within easy view of hell's loathsome gate.

Yet into despair you fired a shaft of grace:
"Forgive and love anew and you will see my face
lined with melancholy pain and strife supernatural;
for you my cross-torn visage still means life eternal."

And so I did forgive and love anew
and even though the pain ceased not but grew
the peace that passes understanding flowered
and we all stand, in your grace empowered

A new man I truly am remade, I can begin
to be as I should have been to you from when
we first were brought together in this world—
but grace says that we may yet rebuild.

I now rededicate my heartful love
to Jesus Christ my Lord who reigns above,
and here on earth to you my love, my leaven,
but for you I may not have seen
the holy gates of heaven.

Dedicated to Sue, January 25, 2002.

A CHRISTMAS ODE TO GIVING

In heaven's great halls of gold
the pillars stand so tall,
and I may stand among them,
since Jesus gave his all.

He gave his life, he gave his soul, he gave his spirit up,
so I may give at Christmas time with a full and cheerful heart.

And not only at Christmas time
but all throughout the year,
when times are hard and God seems far,
I give in holy fear.

What God has given should I withhold,
my selfish heart so mean,
though others rage in bitterness I give,
at peace despite the pain.

For giving is the essence of good,
both in heaven and on earth.
Give and do not count the cost,
recall the cost of the Savior's birth.

Christmas letter 1997, inspired by Joan.

Family

FAMILY AND TRADITION

Family is the tradition that binds a culture together
kinship the spidery glue that bonds families
across the broad spectrum of relationships we call society.
Are we not all of one blood, one ancestor?
Does not every society in every place and time have its place
in one web, framed in the Tree of Life
between the fruits of the knowledge of good and evil?
We tear the fabric of this lovely symmetry at our peril,
we repair the tears with our eccentric patterns to our destruction.
For tradition is the sum of all we know and all we are,
at the point we are.
Tradition is not made by destroying and reinventing tradition.
Tradition grows organically, holistically, intrinsically.
Tradition is a biosocietal rhythm, the dynamic of growth and
rebirth.
Tradition never stays the same because it is simultaneously the
sum of past lives and the vessel of all we are pressing toward.
Tradition holds the promise of everything we ever imagined and
hoped for until now, and the new imaginings and hopes that
spring forth from the amalgam of past desires.
Tradition is a Moebius chain, simultaneously the ground of our
being and the essence of what we will and can be.
Tradition as the sum of past choices, right, wrong and indifferent,
is the great limitation on what we can envision.
Tradition as the vessel of all future choices is the great enabler
that opens vast horizons for exploration and even—creation.
The conservative looking backward sees tradition as the motions
of history which produced his own completeness.
The radical looking forward sees the tradition which will, when
created, produce his own completeness.
The wise are silent before tradition—its weight can crush the
foolhardy who try to tear it down.

The wise are silent before tradition—its fragility will collapse
under those who use it for a bed.
Tradition is a bipolar dynamic—it is the hare we are chasing and
the hound who hunts us down.
So with family. Our roots are inescapable. We must see them
clearly.
Our future is malleable—the way we choose life, the way we face
our deepest fears and loathing,
these choices shape our future and mold the tradition which is
even now ghosting and forming around us.
Choose life.

January 10, 2001

A SONNET TO MY WIFE, OR THE EVOLUTION OF LOVE

When first we love, my love, we burn so hot
a flame of passion rooted in our flesh.
Incandescent light draws us like the moth
cloudless beams in a fast-woven mesh.

And time, the windy enemy of Eros' loves
gutters them from piercing pure to flickering,
drawn by laser light, a fractal art that moves
choices fracture us, or lead into the deepening.

Time, the suffering friend of unconditional love
becomes a window to the faultless light.
We in harmony of dance begin to move
locked as one, unlocking each one's insight.

Finally, we know ourselves, it wasn't us at all,
The great King of Love saved us from the fall.

June 08, 2012

FAITH SONNET FOR ISABELLA EVE

Faith's child by faith came softly to us here
took by surprise and lit a lasting flame
of love eternal, where trust rules, not fear
hearts conjoined, in love for her the same.

And she does grow in spite of worldly pain
taught that good and bad need separation
sheltered from the storms by loving kin
for love finds love and evil loves negation.

Faith's child full grown will not so softly tread
the fiery power of God within her hand
gospel of peace to crush old Satan's head
restoring rightful ownership in this land

So turn and turn again all you who doubt
God's child will ride to battle with trumpet shout.

January 27, 2008.

PEACE SONNET FOR HANNAH GRACE

Graced we are with life, for God has heard us
He sent a gift to make our old faith new,
the peace that dwells within her to redress
the world's sundering, but for a faithful few.

Yet, faithful as ever, peace will follow strife
till eternity condemns old war to death.
The children of God fill the world with life
creation redeemed, as if touched by his breath.

The light of heaven upon her brow a crown
withstanding man's self-inflicted suffering,
though not by any worldly means cast down,
sharing the world's pain, until its liberating.

So if you lack the peace just turn your face
and childlike see the light in Hannah Grace.

October 22, 2010.

JOSHUA JIMMY

Therefore I need gentleness,
by which the ruler of this age is destroyed.

—IGNATIUS OF ANTIOCH

Blessed is he, so born in grace,
of God beloved and loved by all.
He shines before the shining face
preemptively redeemed in full.

To be a blessing, such is he called,
deep in his eyes the Lord looks out,
sensitive soul, touching, feeling all,
yet strong of will, with no doubt.

Grace will lead him on the way
in the armor of righteousness
finding those who chose to stray
reviving many broken spirits.

And gentleness will be his tool
tho' gentle tongue can break a bone
a warrior never plays the fool
he endures until the battle's done.

Through Christ alone he will cast down
our enemy upon the ground
by Joshua he'll see destruction.

May 1, 2014.

A SONNET FOR ZARA EDEN

In Paradise we live positionally
salvation born to blood of royal line
this child's soul preemptively set free
her parents' faith her own faith will refine.

This princess will a shield of light appear
illumining the way, the fallen can stand
protecting all her kindred with the spear
of destiny that Christ puts in her hand.

And from her hand will come the healing grace
that heals the child of God in spirit and truth
for faithful heart will always win the race
and claim the victor's crown even on this earth.

So, Zara Eden welcome and Godspeed
the time when all of us stand with you, freed.

January 5, 2014.

DANIEL KELVIN

Daniel's calm is strength at its very best
in trials and misfortunes and life's joys.
The prophet of old Israel stood the test
and Daniel will not yield to subtle ploys.

Virtue, gravitas, and dignity were signs
of God given authority to ancient world
to those who could draw the boundary lines
heaven's decree established by the word.

This young judge will cause the proud to fear
for clear and prescient judgment is his gift.
Knowledge and power will grow year by year
the light divine healing our fatal rift.

So do not fear but welcome him, God's best,
a river man who'll guide us through the mist.

September 5, 2015.

POPPA'S WORD

Dan, Zara, Josh, Hannah, Isabella we love you, you should know
because this poem tells you so.
We will always be your friend,
with you always to the end,

And Jesus loves you even more,
so quickly now, knock on his door.
He will always let you in,
in him your true life will begin.

June 9, 2022.

A SONNET ON HIS NEW LIFE

Jimmy, not Aubrey thanks, entered this world
A world recovering from the pain of war
War he hated, yet saw another unfurled
His teens the great depression, destined a battler.

But Jim found new life, found a perfect wife
Children multiplied, bouncing baby boomers
Cursed the Beatles, suffered joys of teenage strife
Through Vietnam, Cuba and nuclear rumors.

Then new life found Jim, surprised by Jesus.
The whole family, filled with new faith plunged in,
Signs following, though we struggle still, each of us
steadied by our dad, whose strength was ever . . .
in him

He passes from this world, a new name written
His love and sacrifice for us will never be forgotten.

On my father's passing, Friday, August 5, 2011.

ON HER SEVENTIETH BIRTHDAY

In her childhood came unwilling here
Left England's rain for sunny antipodes
But blessed we were as God would make it clear
For she would meet him with us in this place.

And so through marriage, study and new life
God's hand built our family in love
We turned to him in all our times of strife
A baptism of fire, anointed by the dove.

Life's paradox confronts us all, whatever,
seventeen we feel not seventy
Faith and wisdom grown a little stronger
More time for prayer and loving family.

Youth is not wasted on the young
Nor on the old
Our young spirits are always fresh and strong.

For Sue, June 8, 2018.

IT'S ALL I HAD TIME FOR

Typing my Christmas letter,
Listening to Endorphin play Satie 1,
Reflecting on a year of pleasure and pain,
I remember . . .
I remember . . . love's sweet gifts:
Nola's happy eightieth birthday,
finding pictures of my great grandparents,
those once legendary amorphous figures
now crystalline clear in my photo file,
stored forever? In digital medium, anyway, timeless
in their effect on the generations after them.

The millennium ends,
the millennium begins,
long live the millennium? No!
Long live the people of the millennium,
long live friendship, family, passion and joy,
long life, pleasure and pain lived to the full,
for you.

Christmas, 2000.

TO EVELYN

Empty are the days since your passing
a friendly chat over the phone each night
your company on our mild adventuring
and wisdom when things went not right.

Yet this I still with you in spirit sharing
when near death we both felt the same,
the mighty everlasting arms supporting
assurance that in the end, we go home.

So, farewell my friend, my second mother
until we meet again at the end of days.
May he keep you till we meet, our Savior,
we cannot possibly fathom all his ways.

On Evelyn's death January 18, 2008; written January 23, 2008.

THE PAIN OF LOSS

Pain too deep to know or comprehend
we feel it so
suffering which theology cannot mend
so much we cannot know
only healed by him he chose to send
believe it now
in whose arms our grief will have an end.

September 29, 2014.

FOR LINDA

A light in darkness shines
there at our time of pain
our God who us refines
will show his love again.

It seems no just reward
as in our Lord we stay
yet though the way is hard
he trod a harder way.

We love a God who knows our sorrow
the weal each soul can bear
he knew it before our broken tomorrow
for he first was broken there.

So we live the knife-edge of life
between pain and joy we tread
each step we take can lead to strife
or peace and grace instead.

God is Lord and Jesus King
else darkness rules by insurrection
life forever we keep choosing
day by day each day till resurrection.

October, 1998.

ROSE AND THORN—THORN AND ROSE

When we first loved   we hardly dared believe
our hearts were sealed as one, one mind and spirit together
in love and hope we looked   our old lives did we leave
and saw new life begun   gained the gift forever.

When we began our life   the troubles that began
anew, yet won the race   the hurdles seemed too easy
overcoming each hint of strife we cleared them as we ran
stood firm, face to face   eye to eye stood in victory.

Who turned aside our love?   What enemy us provoked?
to cloud our troubled mind   with thoughts we could
                 prevent

we come to blame and move   inch by inch till separated
apart, as if no longer bound   fear dissolved our heart
                 cement.

For bound we are, inseparate though separate indeed we feel
by bonds not easily undone   yet spirit joined in pledge of
                 honor

unless we tear ourselves apart our souls could break the seal
and bloody, reenter life alone without a thought of grace and
                 power.

We cannot redeem ourselves once fallen into gray despair
only ask for grace to hope not hate though easier to turn
                 away

repentance and forgiveness salves there is a way of peace so near
the deepest wounds of fate   healed by the holy Son's light
                 ray.

Look up, look wide, learn to know for knowledge of the light is
                 there

your well of faith can be outpoured

a deeper love and trust will grow

and life's meaning be restored

a radiant river free to
us
as through our soul flows
fresh, clean air,
for Life always prevails.

March 21, 2010.

FATHER OF MINE

Oh, I wish I'd paid more attention to me dad
his advice doesn't seem half so bad
now that I'm older and a little bit wider
Oh, I wish I'd paid more attention to me dad.

I remember the things that he'd say
passing the time back in the day
when he switched off the TV and poured a beer
Oh, I wish I'd paid more attention to me dad.

The tellie is rubbish, we should throw it out
what's more important is what you're thinking about
and always doing what makes you glad
Oh, I wish I'd paid more attention to me dad.

But I look around at my family now
and I reckon that I am very proud
of what we've all become,
there's no skin off my bum
I guess I did pay attention to me dad!

January 9, 2022.

GERRY

Gerry, daughter of Wyn,
do you love me more than anyone?
Yes, Lord, you know that I love you!
Feed my lambs, be faithful and true.

Geraldine, daughter of Columba,
Do you love me? And my Father?
You know that I love you! Yes Lord!
Tend my sheep, all whom I have called.

Geraldine Winifred, daughter of mine,
Do you love me, till the end of time?
Lord, Holy Spirit, I love you to the end!
Feed my sheep, sustain all those I send.

And Gerry, aunt and sister to many
Gave Christ's life and hope to any
who would simply trust and believe.

Based on John 21:15–18, and Gerry's life.
Written August 12, 2021 and revised on Gerry's death day,
November 25, 2021.

A NEW YEAR'S GREETING

A bright and clear day dawning
awake in clear-eyed prescience
a new and bright year forming
deep hope its effervescence.

Gone are the weeds of mourning
for things that had to end
In flow the tides of cleansing
to the estuary of our mind.

Directions fresh and pioneering
old paths left behind,
we walk and talk while setting
on a path that has no end.

For the road ahead keeps going
to a future we can share
and love can keep on growing
until at last we both come there.

New Year's Day, 2002.

A VISION OF MY PARENTS IN GLORY

I see you now, as you were meant to be
formed in the womb of time, but timeless,
king and queen, alive forever in eternity
powerful, overcoming, interceding for us.

And we commit ourselves to so become
the overcomers we were meant to be
ruling as we may our present home
until we join you, home at last, and free.

October 9, 2011.

Church and Christian Life

THE MANTLE OF MINISTRY

If the mantle comes down from heaven above,
It fits the wearer like a glove,
But if it only comes from human desire,
its purpose is to burn with fire.

Yet God is merciful in his love,
He may shape the wearer to the glove,
Though not for this should we aspire,
but to know his will and his desire.

For man proposes and God disposes,
Man does this and God shapes that,
But the true calling from heaven is divine,
when you hear and answer the mantle is thine.

Circa 1992.

THE YEARS

He chose us in him before the creation of the world!

—EPH 1:4

Anoint the head for healing and empowering
Anoint the years with life, now and everlasting
Wash the soul for peace and his redemption
Wash the years in his stream of consummation.

Let the living waters wash the years away,
we yet fight as one in the righteous fray,
standing as one in that great, that glorious day.

June 7, 2020.

HORIZONS . . .

EXPANDING AND CONTRACTING HORIZONS IN THEO-LOGICAL STUDY.

The First Year . . . The Troubled Mind

Detachment, the curse of the age,
aloofness, the pride of life,
no more evident than in the visible church,
almost entirely detached from the source of life?

Individual detachment, collective isolation,
we are alone in a crowd of insular observers,
some claiming community or corporatisation,
others honest but in despair?

But look, small islands of light,
some have joined themselves to God and the true church.

Theologies which detach everything from its root,
the consequence in the field of the world,
the earth is littered with broken-off branches,
and discarded, detached theologies.
Theologians who exist, only to . . . scrounge
off a corrupt system which should have rejected them long ago,
but which is so detached from reality
it gave them another degree instead.

But look, small islands of light,
a remnant has believed, in God and his church.

Behold, the word was detached from itself,
the hard bits exorcised by the scalpels of apostate physicians,

and reassembled (if not discarded)
with blunt needle and rough thread,
by those who profess to believe still.

Historical scepticism or historical faith, in the Word,
combine a positive with a negative and you get . . . what you
deserve,
Dis-integrate the word with higher critical analysis and
faithlessness,
and you get lifeless form and the modern barely visible church.

But look, small islands of light,
some still have faith, in God's word, for his church.

A theology which learns its trendy tenets from the world,
ungrounded in creation reality and the natural polarities,
soon discarded.
Those who learn it are left with the handful of pebbles,
gravel between their teeth,
distantiated then fused in a horizon of compromise.

How can we fuse the distantiated elements of our gospel,
into a horizon of blessing and promise . . . What we need!
How can we integrate the words of life into the Word of Life
and become reattached branches, part of the whole tree.

But look, small islands of light,
what man could not do or be, the Holy Spirit is.

The Second Year . . . Reassembling the Pieces

Friend, you are reassembling the pieces of the jigsaw,
I see your new picture emerging,
at least as coherent as the old,
perhaps more so . . . and yet, lacking perspicuity?

Brother, I saw your anxious looks, I observed the creases of
worry,
the intense concentration of a man,
troubled and searching to the depths of his soul,
but now you seem focused, certain and decided.

And yet you have become an island to me,
your innocent freedom is gone, lost in self-authentication?

Are you still my friend, or are you to become my foe,
in some future time when our reassembled pictures are found to
be . . . inherently different.
Have our horizons fused around a different center?
And yet is not Jesus and his word the only center for us?

O my brother, I tremble
when I hear your confident theological assertions,
so different now
to the simplicity of the faith you once had (or did you?)
Plenty of conviction but lacking life,
soundly constructed and intensely rational, but somehow
demeaning to the ordinary saint.
And so have I become an island to you,
the foundations of our faith set in different soil?

O my soul, dare I compare myself to my brother,
look instead to your own picture,
reassembled from the scattered fragments of your mind.
Did you retain the correct pieces,

did you reassemble correctly the image of Christ?

Look now my soul, at the image you have assembled,
reflect now my mind the word of the Lord.
Fuse your horizon with his, guard against those with no clear
vision,
be sure only of your own salvation.

Lord, could I have become an island to you,
integrated into the jigsaw of the world's hermeneutic?

The Third Year . . . Who Can Be Saved?

"Always begin with what you know," said Holmes,
"otherwise you'll end up knowing nothing,"
which might be good if you're a Zen Buddhist or a Scientologist,
but not if you're a Christian preacher.

Perhaps we should rephrase for Sherlock, and say,
always begin with *who* you know, especially in learning about
God.
If we begin with Jesus, we can't go far wrong, can we?
And yet some have made shipwreck of their faith.

Lord, save me from becoming an island to you,
isolated by the shifting sands of other men's doctrines.

But how do I know that I know . . . that I know?
Must I choose between functional authority of the Word, de
facto,
and the revelation authority of the Word, *de jure*?
I might spiral forever downward between the two, *de profundis*.

What is the key that will make the spiral go upward?
Is it the opinion of super-reader?

Propositional content but no transformative power.
Is it the opinion of the charismatic preacher who believes what he
says and says what he believes? Transformative power (maybe)
but no propositional content.
Is there a key at all?

Lord I have lost the key to my Chateau d'If,
help me escape from this island prison.

Now there is a key if you dare to take it.
Someone will die and you will be cast out of prison in his place.
So, someone has died and my old prisoner self has been clothed
in his grave rags,
Now I may be cast forth to freedom, and with a map to find an
inestimable treasure.

So, the work of God is revealed in a death, his authority
established in a cross toward which the Word pointed
and from which the Word shows the way.
Therefore, I must begin from God's *de jure* authority,
established in his Word,
as it was in the beginning . . . *de fide.*

Lord show me by your Spirit how to swim,
and deliver me from sharks in the hermeneutical pool.

My starting point then,
not that our reception of the Word may give it authority,
making a meaningless introversion,
but that I receive the Holy Spirit of the Word
and submit myself to his call to expand my horizon,
in conformity with him and the Word he enlivens . . .
Without Pentecost there is no valid hermeneutic!

The Holy Spirit is the key, faith is the turning in the lock.
The only truly fundamental hermeneutical principle—

relationship with God through Jesus Christ our Lord,
the choices of faith God's hermeneutic of us!
Who can tell but he
who will pass the test.

Lord give me your Spirit. Lord give me the gift of faith.
Only you can give the gift of peace.

Hermeneutics class, 1992.

WHO IS THIS WOMAN?

I must perceive
The true pulse of her existence—what she really is
The true purpose of her being—why she is
The true purpose of her becoming—what she will be.

The true pulse of her existence is to serve others through
Empathic understanding
Empowering knowledge
Soul strengthening.

The true purpose of her being is to link severed bonds between
People and their spirit
People and their world
People and their God.

The true purpose of her becoming—
she will be
is and is becoming
A true creature of holy light.

A righteous archon of indescribable beauty and power
A friend of God and humankind.

Late 2001.

A PASSOVER EASTER

Pesach, the death of the lamb
Remember our deliverance
Angel of death pass over us
Who spared Isaac for a ram
And Moses' people by the blood
As Noah's family from the flood
So we worship the great I am
By his sacrifice we're set free
Holy priests and kings are we
Jew and Gentile one new man.

15N 5779/April 19, 2019.

THE CHRISTMAS HANUKKAH YEAR

Four times in a hundred years, it's not often we come together
Jew and Gentile celebrating with one another
Just a step in history, or type and reality of Salvation?
thus, victory for a nation which enabled cosmic redemption.
The lights burn, how they burn now and forever
The victory of arms subsumed, in the arms of a mother,
Jewish son of a Jewish mother, worth a celebration
Yet a life well lived seemed to end in degradation?
The answer, now and always,
Anointed times, anointed peoples,
Choose life, care not for global troubles
Circumcision of the heart
is what the season's really all about.

2016

A CHRISTMAS AND HANUKKAH SONNET

After oppression comes the light of freedom
attendant waits to usher freedom in
brave men fought and died to make it welcome
the house is now sanctified and swept clean.

Into accusing darkness came the light
a false king threatened in all self-glory
in vain folly he tries to snuff it out,
but miracle of light makes another story.

My temple restored, redeemed new birth
a Savior who fulfilled the prophecies
a high priest who could holy rule the earth
would be celebrated for two thousand years.

And he will come in glory yet again
to save his people and rule Jerusalem.

2015

THE CHRISTIAN WARRIOR

However hard it gets, however much the pain
The warrior rises to his feet, ever and again.
And though one day our strength will fail
when we can barely lift our head
The one who makes the desert bloom
will be our strength instead.

See, I am doing a new thing!
Now it springs up; do you not perceive it?
I am making a way in the wilderness and streams in the wasteland.
—Isa 43:19

November 20, 2020.

THE WAY

Trust in the Lord with all your heart and lean not on your own understanding.

PROV 3:5

The narrow way is narrowing
The rough path gets rougher
But the gates of heaven shine brighter
And the heavenly song rings louder.

January 15, 2010.

THE PATH

The path leads on through joys and sorrows
yet light is given when the path is dark.
A narrow way leads me to the hallows
the arrow flies true till it hits the mark.

HEARING LIGHT

When Simeon and Clara were wed
the moon rose bright and clearest
and over the valley hills bled
the red setting sun from the west.

Now Clara and Simeon are forever
together their light will be strong
the moonlight and sunshine together
will make their partnership long.

When Simeon and Clara look back
they will see a hard road walked aright
no troubles or joys did they lack
as at last they walk into the light.

March 13, 2010.

ELIHU SAW!

*But Elihu . . . became very angry with Job for justifying himself
rather than God.*

—*Job 32:2*

Elihu saw our fault,
in a man as pure could be
A man of pain who suffered all
Before the time of Calvary's tree.

Because our fault is old as sin
Even Job could fall its prey
Encoded in our every gene,
We just don't know the way.

We weigh our fault against our good
And think we have done well,
yet Scripture which should be our food
Consigns such thought to hell.

So even when we're born again
And should know that much better
We look too much to mourn our pain
As though God should be kinder.

We justify ourselves, not Jesus
Who is worthy of all praise
We think our good should safeguard us
No pain should mar our days.

But justify means *righteousing*
and even Paul as a man of sin
at his height of power and working

could scarcely take it in.

"I, worst of sinners among you all,"
And his judgment was not astray
For the more we know and yet still fall
The greater the price to pay.

But Paul knew the key to unlock heaven
he never bemoaned his fate.
He suffered, struggled with continual pain
declaring "God is great."

He knew the struggle that flesh inherits
it can't exist on its own.
We all need quickened, righteous spirits
under the Spirit on the throne.

God is good, holy and just
But about as tame as a lion.
He will tear apart self-righteousness
That stops us being like him.

So when you get to complaining
about the burden you have to bear,
who are you justifying?
If yourself, not God, show fear,

or in fear you will go to your dying.

January 12, 1999.

HATRED **AND HOPE**

Unbearable pain,   No hope for that other, the always-enemy
the hate of millennia   hate that allows no wider human vision
crushes the mind into submission   the willing unwitting vector
mashes emotions into bleeding catatonia   of an unholy miasma.
          who can comprehend the dark malevolence? Soul-churning
     Deepest melancholy, beyond all anger love transmutes despair
Past forgiveness, mercy, remission   with God we walk together
     The hate of millennia consumed by grace, a spiritual rendition
unbearable pain,   filled with all hope for every once-was enemy.

December 28, 2013.

SUFFERING AND HOPE

Suffering is the lot of the guilty fallen
Angels, us, all of his creation.
We seek to mitigate it far too often
even to our faithful God's rejection.

But pain cannot touch the untouchable
Unless he chooses to make himself amenable
To share the abyss which looms inevitable
for us, destruction unto life or death eternal.

Hope in suffering is the prayer of the guilty fallen
All creation waits in holy expectation
To leap the dark abyss our enemy has riven
Falling into the light graciously given.

If grace to endure the unspeakable is given to the faithless
Will the faithful conquer less?

December 28, 2013.

IF I FORGET

If I forget your cross, my holy Lord
mindful not of your body's resurrection,
my future hope cannot be seen assured,
and I fail to find the Lord of all creation.

If you come not to us in that last day
Why did you come to us through Mary's womb?
If I approach not your glorious body
I seal your cross-torn body in the tomb.

If you created not the heavens and earth,
how can there ever be a New Jerusalem?
But I embrace our need for the new birth,
and live to be a part of the one new man.

November 11, 2020.

FORGET WHAT IS BEHIND

One thing I've done
I've forgotten what is past
I strive for what lies farther on
I press on at last.

I race on toward the goal
God has called me heavenward,
I press on to win the prize
in Jesus Christ, my Lord.

Phil 3:13–14; February 25, 1992.

FREEDOM IS RELATIVE

Bound in the chains of their freedom,
fools mock the wisdom of the wise,
found out in the consequence of sin,
yet waits their great doom, the great assize.

2022

HOLINESS, OR GOD'S LOVE AND OUR LOVE

The holiness words, like separation,
righteousness and led by the Spirit,
wisdom, hope, and faith without limit-
are true enough, but not enough,
for our great commission.

It is love that marks our separation
our love for God and his loving Spirit.
Wisdom, hope and faith have their limit
so without love in our hearts
it's a foolish mission.

The mission of God is restoration,
love that was, before we lost our spirit
in love we are wise, hope and believe it
it's the holiness of love
(not the love of holiness)
that fulfills our mission.

January 15, 2010.

ONLY BELIEVE

Only believe the Word of God,
Only believe, only believe.
Better to believe and later find,
belief in part misdirected.
Relieve the burden of your soul,
be made whole,
for God in justice will exact the toll,
for those in unbelief, no hope at all.

Believe what is right, believe what is true, amen.
He has told us the truth and shown us righteousness,
there is no excuse, O faithless world of man.
You who show no mercy, cruel, hard eyed, ruthless
Your logic and your reason damn the truth to hell,
Bright stoic light, narcissi, truth to tell
that light is darkness visible, doom fell.

O Anacreon,
How can I bear your hateful lusts
Falsely proclaimed as honourable loves.
Repent and believe the truth
reject the lies of hell and death
light of God penetrates any depth!

Inspired by Geoffrey T. Bull, *A New Pilgrim's Progress,* **chapter 6;
March 3, 2019.**

UNITY AND DISCORD

The unity of Christmas past
was it an illusion which we held fast
for so long?
It seemed that we were free,
albeit for one brief season
of forgiveness, grace and love.

But now, is that time gone for good?
trumpeted out of mind and heart
by heartless trumped-up charges
against each other,
unforgiveable that you,
of all people,
should support that reckless wreck
of false, oh, entirely conditioned beliefs,
brain-washed tropes of an unthinking world.

Yes, it's him I am talking about,
surrendered without a shout,
babe to tortured Savior.
He forgave, no conditions,
forgive them, they know not what they do,
they do and cannot know
forgiveness, grace and love
unless it starts with us,
in the unity of a Christmas present—
and yet to come.

Christmas, 2017

A CHRISTMAS FAITHFUL AND TRUE

Faithful, yes, faithful and true,
Christ emptied himself for me and for you,
born of our flesh and our blood,
and laid to rest in a humble abode.

Yet the word went to rich and to poor men,
to wise and to humble of mind,
both responded to what they were given,
by our Lord who is merciful and kind.

Faithful to the light they were given,
the wise men traveled far by their lore,
true to the heavenly leading,
they came at last to the Christ child's door.

They worshiped him and they adored,
He would save the whole world by his love,
gifts and worship they offered their Lord,
and they did not betray him to Herod.

Yet other wise men saw the same sign—
they knew where he was born and would die,
but they betrayed him and allowed the crucifixion,
which kind of wise man am I?

Poor men heard the news through a vision,
their knowledge was not great or profound,
but they obeyed the heavenly commission,
and on that night the Christ child was found.

They saw the child wrapped in rags in a manger,
they spread the word of their Savior and Lord,
though their words seemed to others far stranger,

his mother in her heart kept them stored.

Surely other shepherds heard of this vision,
the pastors of the flock of Israel,
but they would not believe in his mission,
when I do likewise, I hammer in the nail.

He will come again in glory to judge all of us,
not humbly but in majesty and power,
we will kneel at his throne and his name confess,
when the Lord is revealed in that hour.

Faithful, yes faithful and true,
like him I empty myself for you.
Brothers and sisters by torn flesh and spilled blood,
together we'll partake of his heavenly food.

June 12, 1993.

God, The Beloved

FAITH SONNET ON THE ONENESS OF GOD

Three lines extend throughout the universe
create our three dimensions, sense of place
so they meet in singularity diverse
the measurement which some think to embrace.

But our great Father drew the prime meridian
fixed the music of the spheres in our heart
but rule of love our soul's consideration
lest cold reason stumble our stumbling start.

Sure enough, it did, helped by a son
of perdition, but Holy Flame held another
Son of Man, in whom the heavenly battle won
one who could also claim a Jewish mother.

Third line meets our image, in the Spirit free
body soul and spirit united spiritually.

December 21, 2009.

SONNET ON THE LORD JESUS

Time was when time was not, a contradiction.
He was, when we were not, Lord of all—Glory!
Love-conceived past the womb of time, no fiction
inscribed his plan for us, an unwritten-written story.

Us-perfect came, humble servant to the cross
end of childhood, child came in lowly splendor
whip-weary, we looked askance, as at outcast dross
then, blinded by light, wounds healed,
our outlaw all redeemer.

We walk by faith not sight, sense his Paraclete
in this age of last things, his presence lost not less
Spirit-guiding, Spirit-leading our heart-soul incomplete
yet within, fills our spirit, with all his all-completeness.

Surprising he will be, great King in Jerusalem
powers cast down, us-exalted, established in shalom.

January 15, 2010.

THE LION'S CLAW

All the fearful essence concentrated
Curved, sharp, steel-pointed,
Extension of muscular power,
tense to spring.
Giant shoulders flex, eye fixed
Prey unwary turns its back
Nameless shadow still and poised
Shadows of foliage, leaf and branch
Merge within the camouflage of death
Whole body springs, focused
One sharp pointed powerful claw enough
To bring the creature to the ground,
Fate certain, life gone, no mercy here!

And yet, he said, I will forgive
Your life is not forfeit.
Though you are cut down
I will raise you up,
the claws are sheathed,
take my hand.

October 20, 2020.

SWORDS

Swords of grace and law, justice and mercy

Lux
Lucifer
Evilalive
Michael
In heaven
The sword
Of the Lord
vs Satan
Darkness
Visible
Ejected
Rejected
To hell with you!
Destroy your world!
The sword of no avail
lies destroyed our Paradise
The flaming swords of Cherubim define our fall from grace
The penalty of our sin, a world as hard and cold as ice
The sword which cast
Devil out from heaven
Cold & hard, 2-edged
Cuts both ways in an
Argument, truth told.
Tempered each blade,
Righteous and not so,
biter bitten & knows
pain of choices made
in untempered heart.
Abraham tempered &

Became God's sword.
In Canaan Salem saw
Elam cast down low,
Abram paid the tithe.
Israel became sword
Nations in the forge.
Sword of the Lord &
Gideon, & David took
enemy's great blade,
but took his head too.
Man of blood (Uriah),
couldn't build temple.
In a place of sacrifice.
no noise of iron heard
until power of the state
exceed a due authority.
A place for the people,
not people for the place,
sacrifice forsaken, gain,
Mammon replace grace,
& legalised lust ends
crucifying the just.
Christ-born babe
Life of service
To the King
Repent for
Kingdom
At hand
Nail &
spear
Abi
V
✝

A
Iam
Risen
Adamic
stigmatic
Immortal
Repent for
King is come
serve him only
Christ-born babe
Crucify the old man
For the legal penalty of
our own sin paid in full
God's son the world does
to death before his time,
yet, before time he said,
thus it must be done! All
has been fulfilled, so you,
look, he makes all things
New, now, & in eternity.
Eternity begins, back to
the future & forward on
to an infinity of service,
Yet how few will serve,
& we, band of brothers
as marked for death &
martyrdom, surrender
to him who set us free,
life, limbs, soul & spirit
forged in fire, alloyed in
each other's steel, edge
to cut and be cut clean
thru' joints and marrow
discerning thought and
heart intention, Spirit of
God, moving through &

through us, building the
Church eternal, a bride.
The bride which is and
will be, just as he is the
One who is and who was
and who will be, eternity
awaits we who patiently
endure the pain he did.
Rejection of those earth
dwellers who cannot see,
self & Devil blinded they
miss the obvious signs of
their doom approaching.
And so the judgments begin, Seal, Trumpet and Bowl
Flaming Swords of Michael and Cherubim, define Satan's fall
Down to earth then down to the lake
of fire, share not their
eternal pain, come out
it's not too late,
Repent, be
Accepted,
Cleansed
By fire
if need
be, but
know the
healing tree
eternal, man
immortal,
Seize the
New
Life!

January 31, 2021

COMMITMENT PRAYER

Lord,

Let me see your guidance, with the eyes of your Holy Spirit
let me know your strength, with certainty and without limit
with fear, trembling I advance, let me overcome by your grace
with power, in faith I go forth, lead me in love to see your face.

April 12, 2010, while doing Cleansing Stream devotions.

INTO THE LIGHT

Dark it seems and darker still it's getting
And looking back looks darker yet, until
Moving and moved on we go regretting,
hoping we come to the end of that tunnel.

The bright light may dazzle us temporarily
but soon enough our eyes fix on the goal,
we soon overcome every obstacle we see,
no fear or dread can impede us at all.

In this life and the next we go on in faith,
courage and blessing found only in his Christ.

2022

Last Days

CAUGHT IN A NET OF DREAMS

As sinking in the depth of night
My thought in spirit runs
I catch a dream as in a net
A vision of the world to come.

A savage world that will emerge
In civil strife of global reach
Across the bounds of nations surge
The call to hate; O brother, speak.

But none can speak except to hate
They do not know the way of love
For who could teach, it is too late,
Murdered, are the children of God.

For law becomes a graceless wight
Spawning fools who hate the light of grace.
Destroyed the souls of lovers of the light
the world left, a dark and dreary place.

And in that dark what else could flower
But fearful, deep divided opinion
When right belongs to the greatest power
Briefly triumphant, before its self-destruction.

What hope there is rests not in us, it's clear
Nor in false prophets, nor Antichrist
But only through inbreaking, invasion from the air
The King of Glory, setting all to right.

Midnight, May 28, 2005. The world after the tribulation; it hovers on our doorstep.

SONG OF THE BELOVED, OR THE EPIC OF THE ESCHATON

As God is gracious, what I say rings true,
long have I lived, known by many names,
hiding in the shadows, and loved by very few,
even with those I love, forced to play games,
until they moved on and I, living on
unsmiling, lost souls shrouding my vision,
till I, poor redeemed soul,
could help them to contrition.

And so I was, in the spirit, waiting,
on him who redeemed my life forever,
saw a messenger of God descending
full radiance of light from light together,
a trumpet voice sounded, not yet the last
commanding me, hold each word fast,
so that I, poor enlightened seer
might give them to the saints sans fear.

Saw I did, in a perpetual flash untimely,
events unfolded, it seemed a death dream,
unraveling together in what was eternity.
One moment could have filled a ream,
even the silence lasting half an hour
filled with wisdom, grace and power,
sweet in my mouth, in my belly sour,
until I, poor and overwhelmed in spirit
saw clearly, plain prose could not fulfill it.

Heard plainly, though born deaf, ears open,
I am the Word, speak in golden prophecy,
things that have been, are and will be shown.

I am the door, open and write in silver poesy.
Words and knowledge may open doors,
but mystery words contain many a thesis,
to wisely give and withhold access,
anointed, poor, unworthy I, set down
words, gifted from God's gracious throne.

In the beginning, in the beginning the Word is,
light was, and darkness twisted from it.
Bearer of light became visible darkness
and we, O foolish twisted us, followed,
half-heartedly, whimpering to our death,
hating, embracing the bloody scythe,
outside our lost home of hope we writhe,
until darkness be untwisted, and light
shine again, offering his eternal rest.

Resurrection from the dead, birth pains,
deception, war, pestilence, famine,
bitter hearts prevent more resurrections.
The earth shakes and sorrows begin,
Yet the true blood cannot be denied,
He was once for all unjustly tried,
by grace and faith those who died
across millennia paved a narrow way,
preparing for that great and glorious day.

The time is soon, difficult labor at hand,
the faithful slain as persecution deepens.
Deception by the false prophetic band,
false kisses from our erstwhile brothers.
The love of most grows frosty cold,
The earth seems grim and very old,
yet witnesses endure, patience untold.
They will be taken up in glory, yet unseen
first the stage is set in his high heaven.

Lamb worthy to open the judgment scroll,
none else in heaven nor below on earth,
we thank God that only Christ reveals
what's been declared since creation's birth.
Emerald rainbow, bloodstones and thrones,
thunder, lightning, seven fiery lamps,
elders Jew and Gentile cast down crowns,
for he alone is worthy of all praise,
To open the scroll and loosen all its seals.

The prayers of the saints rise as incense,
elders and angels praise the great redeemer,
everything in heaven and on earth gives voice.
So you, fall down and worship him forever,
for worthy is the Lamb who was slain,
in his high kingdom neither death nor pain.
All is ready, the great finale will soon begin,
few the elect though great in number
living and dead will rise in hidden rapture.

Watch then, knowing not his perfect time!
Be holy, faithful, true and persevering,
the remnant are not any who vainly claim
kinship with the Lord but unbelieving.
Lest he come when you are all unready,
to escape what comes to pass unworthy
not walking in the Spirit, but found sleepy.
He will keep from the hour of trial so near,
if in his command we faithful persevere.

And battle on we must for the Beast arises,
can any flesh be saved from his dread master?
Yet those dark days, though dire, God shortens,
mortal wound is healed and war follows after,
against the elect, impressed with angelic seal.
Leopard, Bear, Lion, jaws and claws of steel,

bowing to the Dragon who made his head to heal.
False peace he offers so he might be worshiped,
till time is up and his true face revealed.

Desolating abomination in the holy place,
covenant of false peace cast aside midweek,
sacrifice to God replaced by the idolatrous
worship and self-worship he will seek.
His armies of fear surround the holy city
All faithful who resist receive no pity
Into the place prepared they can but flee.
Yet there will be at last a consummation
poured out quickly on all his desolation.

The great red dragon will ultimately fail,
carried to refuge in the air the glorious lady,
his purpose to destroy the children of Israel
foiled, as earth and heaven make conspiracy.
Earth swallows flood, manna falls from heaven,
though in rage he wars against their brethren,
Michael yet protects God's messianic children.
O witness all these things our Lord above
And raise your martyred saints to the throne of love.

For times, time and half a time deep tribulation
intensifies as the scroll's unsealed.
White, red, black, pale, the horses of destruction
go forth to wreak fair judgment on the world,
and the tribulation saints, yet unsealed
feel the force of Antichrist unleashed
his rage in a judgment of death revealed.
So their souls lie under the altar of God
robes whitened in the Lamb's blood.

False Christ and false prophet, speaking fair
but acting foul, mouths open in blasphemy,

the faithful who have heard show no fear,
though condemned to sword and captivity.
You are forewarned, my people, show patience,
though an idol image speaks false pretense,
be not deceived by mammon's pseudoscience.
Doomed are the lawless sons of perdition
by His fiery breath, the brightness of His coming.

The trumpet has been sounded, no excuse
Sign in the sky, look! the eagles gather
Not in the desert nor in the inner rooms
An angel flying in the heavens will declare
Babylon is fallen, O how it all falls dark.
Glory to the Ancient of Days, do his work,
unless you worship the Beast with his mark.
They will drink the wine of God's wrath,
in their tormented haze no saving path.

Sixth seal, light of heavens withdrawn
all nations distressed, What is to come?
the twisted hosts to earth cast down,
more fearful yet of the wrath of the Lamb.
Earth quakes yet they hide in a cave,
no cry of repentance, yet deliverance crave
to sinful hopes they ingloriously cleave.
Islands will move and mountains will fall,
but they refuse worship to the Lord of all.

And a cross will appear in high heaven
the Son of Man in the clouds will appear.
Quickly, humble yourselves, O men
to redemption you may still draw near.
But if you cling to your shaming of the Son,
you will be lost though the battle has been won
Doomed to your judgment of destruction.
He comes in like manner as he had gone,

but his work in the heavens is not done.

First work when he comes in the clouds,
to summon the faithful remnant,
all who remain from the killing fields,
and every dead beheaded saint
raptured openly to their Lord on high.
The tribes of Israel can no longer deny
their true Messiah. Weeping they sigh,
death is swallowed up in life and victory,
many turn from the beast to the Son of Glory,
receiving the seal of God to turn his fury.

Then, the seventh seal, unsealed in silence,
we cannot know its hidden import,
but the seven trumpets with much incense
are the heartfelt prayers of every saint.
Noise, thunderings, lightnings, the earth quakes
again, even before the first trumpet speaks,
repent, the trumpets are the final chance!
En masse, Messiah's people rally at the sound,
but will the Gentile nations turn around.

Hail, fire and blood, a third of trees and grass,
great fiery mountain, a third of the bloody sea,
Wormwood burns a third of all fresh waters,
sun, moon, stars a third darkened in the day.
Woe, woe, woe to earth's inhabitants,
as angel key unlocks the deep abyss,
the seal of God from scorpions protects,
yet a vast eastern horde kills a third of man
and still sorcery, murder, theft and fornication.

The rainbow angel stands on land and sea,
face like the sun, feet like pillars of fire,
He cries out, the seven thunders reply

yet sealed from us in measure.
Eat the little scroll from the angel's hand
bitter sweet to take the prophetic stand
for time, times and half a time around
when the holy people are completely broken,
and our enemies believe that they have won.

Second work as he abides high in the clouds,
to send his ambassadors, plenipotentiary
perhaps the seven thunders spoke their names.
Two witnesses in power and fiery testimony
shut up the heavens, turn waters into blood,
fighting against all that hell-spawned brood.
The holy rally to them, to do or die in love,
yet before the last and seventh trumpet sound
all saints and both witnesses are destroyed.

O how they celebrate, Beast and his slavery,
they dishonor the dead, those holy, just and true.
In Sodom and Egypt, brief, pyrrhic victory,
true church seems gone, but always lives anew,
especially in that city where he bled and died,
earthquake, thousands die, one tenth destroyed
they give grudging glory to heaven's high God.
In fear they hear the seventh trumpet sound
they know now, soon they will be judged.

The judge, Son of Man, appears again on high
reaps with the sickle, enthroned upon the cloud,
signaling final judgment bowls are nigh,
and the winepress overflows with deep red blood.
The bowls of wrath are poured out quickly
sores for marked men, waters turn bloody,
not one third but all the waters filthy,
and in their thirst the sun scorches with fire,
but none repent, cursing God in reckless ire.

Sixth angel's bowl poured out, fierce wine
Dragon, Beast and prophet spew false spirits
all the earth summoned to their destruction
at Armageddon, their shame open, no garments,
naked and drunk, they stand before his wrath.
Noise, thunderings, lightnings, the earth
quakes as never before, signal the seventh
the city splits in three, the nations' cities fall,
Babylon will fall, giant hailstones, and still
they blaspheme God!

Mystery, Babylon the Great, Mother of Harlots
supported by corrupt rulers of this age,
poured out and reveled in her abominations,
destroying her children in the bloody pillage.
The Beast's kings will tear her limb from limb
consumed with fire, desolate and naked,
God willed it, the words of God fulfilled.
Her fall has been announced from age to age,
Come out now! lest you share in her every plague.

The seventh trump has sounded
The bowls have been poured out
The harlot has been judged
The saints rise with a shout
The Amen has been sounded,
the Hallelujah called,
the saints for battle all well-armed,
everyone a rider clothed in white,
even as their captain, who leads them in the fight.

His marriage supper's ready,
The feasting before the war,
for there is one outcome only,
victory, to the holy and the pure.

He refines like launderer's soap
for the unclean Beast there is no hope.
They do not fear me says the Lord of the Host.
He drinks the fruit of the vine in those days,
and in his Father's kingdom we sing praise.

At last the King returns in power
on a white horse, faithful and true,
righteous judge and maker of war,
a name written that no one knew.
His robe is dipped in blood, the Word of God
God's armies white clothed, his mouth a sword
He is the King of kings and of all lords the Lord.
All carrion birds are summoned to the feast,
the flesh of all his foes, both small and great.

Oh, you who hear come out this very hour,
learn to obey the gospel of our Lord,
before he vengeance takes in flaming fire
and you destroyed by the glory of his power.
His feet will stand, the Mount of Olives split,
and every saint will stand with him on it,
the year of God's redeemed has come to comfort,
so all his faithful children in Jerusalem
drink deeply the consolation of her bosom.

Knowing their doom but stubborn to admit
their crimes and sins of idol worship
they cling to their allegiance to the Beast
by the False Prophet, deceived and self-deceived.
Vast armies avail them nothing from his ire
Beast and False Prophet, the seditious pair
Cast alive into the brimstone lake of fire,
their followers die by the rider's sword,
a faithful judgment feast for every bird.

So that old serpent is bound down in chains,
Satan laid so low in dishonor,
bound for a thousand years in the Abyss
the key turned, no more to play deceiver.
Judgment is given to those upon the thrones,
no mark of Beast upon their heads or hands,
living and reigning with Christ a thousand years.
Blessed and holy those in the first resurrection
priests of God and Christ in the last millennium.

Now when the thousand years have expired
the age-old hater, Satan, deceives again.
Mystery of deception, to battle they are gathered
Gog-Magog, many from every nation.
One thousand years of light not enough for all,
the reprobate prefer darkness though in thrall,
till fire comes from heaven in great hail.
The adversary cast at last into the lake of fire,
tormented day and night forevermore.

So comes the great harvest and separation
saints' and sinners' souls must judgment face
stand naked and alone at the great white throne
book of works and the Book of Life in place.
Did you give me food when I was hungry
or give me drink when I was thirsty
Welcomed me, a naked stranger, clothed me?
Depart to punishment eternal or eternal life
as you may or may not be the Groom's good wife.

With Death and Hades now in the lake of fire
Time for a new heaven and new earth
First heaven and earth and even the sea expire
As New Jerusalem descends in a new birth.
Not the flood which covered all the world
But with fervent heat the elements unfold

And creation begins anew in shining gold.
Behold the destruction of all liars, every coward,
they only prepared the way for the bride.

The holy Jerusalem, great city, descends out of heaven
Light of precious stones, God's glory, clear as crystal.
Twelve tribes and twelve apostles, the one new man
inscribed on the gates and foundations of the wall.
Pearls carved for gates, streets like gold transparent
Every precious stone adorns its fundament
No need for sun and moon, the Lamb its light.
The pure river, the water of life proceeds from his throne
No more curse, leaves of healing, for all who are his own.

The Lord God of the holy prophets has spoken,
keep the words of this his prophecy, worship him.
He is Alpha and Omega, beginning and the end,
prophecy unsealed, and gone is the enemy's time.
Let him who thirsts take the water of life freely
Be not of those who love and practice the lie.
He testifies and says, "Surely, I come quickly."
Believe the Word, don't take from or add to it,
Amen, even so, Come, Lord Jesus Christ!

2021–2022

THE FINAL REJECTION

Come friend, admit the heavy burden on your back,
Confess the wrong you did to place it there
Turn to Christ who took it on the rack
Only confess your need, give no hard stare.

*Yet you did not repent when the gospel was offered freely to you,
with all hard proofs from life and the Word itself, you still rejected
his offer!*

The time has come for the saints to disappear
trumpet call is heard by them, not thee.
Though you see others believe and share
you love your prison too much to be set free.

*You did not repent when the saints were taken from the earth in
hidden rapture, their disappearance and their nature evidence
enough, nor when others revived their dead faith and many others
believed because the Scriptures were fulfilled, yet still you rejected
the gospel!*

An open heaven will reveal the Lord, cross-torn
His saints rise openly to be with Christ
Blinding light and glory take them in
But you instead believe the Antichrist.

*You did not repent when I openly appeared in the heavens and
openly took my saints to be with me. My wounds and my glory
were not enough for you; you still rejected the gospel.*

The sign of the Son of Man remains above
But you prefer false signs from the False Prophet.
The two great witnesses proclaim my love,

they call in truth and power, yet you mock it.

*You did not repent when I sent my two witnesses to testify to you, in
all fire and power of speech, with all proofs from my Word, you saw
and you heard but still you rejected the gospel.*

The world has been destroyed before your eyes
Not least the material world, old Babylon.
Armies of saints and angels fill the skies,
only judgment seat waits after the millennium.

*You destroyed or permitted the destruction of all my saints, last of
all my two witnesses, and you rejoiced in their destruction and your
rejection of the gospel—now know this, I reject you in the war you
brought upon your own heads and I reject you now. Depart forever
into the place prepared for you.*

June 12, 2020.

The World, Nature, and Life

PEOPLE AND PLACES

People are like places because

Sometimes they are distant
And sometimes they are close.
Sometimes they are separated by vast oceans
Yet the culture of their heart and mind is one.

And sometimes teachers and students are like that
Separated by the chasm of the generation gap
Yet sharing a common understanding and joy of life.

Written for Ngaire's school remembrance book, 1996.

THE BIRD OF PARADISE

Foolish to believe in such a gift,
radiant in beauty and glory,
as it flies, heart and spirits lift.
That song tells us another story,
than the worldly sad one.

Why should such a lovely creature be?
Some see no use, discounting love,
losing the essence of life in harmony,
fearing the gentleness of harmless dove,
the world-weary sad ones.

But let my heart sing joy, it will endure
in counterpoint to beauty and to love,
that fills creation with its living splendor.
Iridescent light does shift and move
the world full of us gladsomes.
And I for one am glad you are my friend.

June, 2008.

WAITĀKERE AVATARS

Time before

The sea, brooding in ancient time, held our fated days.
No Tasman Sea then, just vastness of foam flecked green
covering fire and rock resting in a sulfurous haze
fire and water conglomerate, an igneous Miocene.

Earth-writhed, water-carved, land moved up then down
epochal change, slow but sure—we look, frail avatars
through electronic eyes, mock turehu in our town
disconnected from the paradise bequeathed us.

Great it was, our place, green hills flowing to the sea
Parthenon giants stood, roots deep down to last all time,
locked in their island sanctuary, songbirds sweet decree
we are here, here we remain, in this happy clime.

Came the cold, fall and rise again of oceans warming
unsettled but secure alone, the land remained, waiting.

Iwi

First contact, foreborn iwi, appeared on this horizon
old spirit breathing on the land perceived, wait over.
New energy had come, hopeful life, in expectation
walked the land, claimed for their own, and those after.

For centuries the land gave of its best, in harmony
stood the human test, yielded to stone tool and thankful heart.
Though turehu vanished west, prophetic mystery
people of the land knew grace, of thankful land a part.

But none may weather time so well, unscathed by war,
we till the land, think it owned, yet others rise, make claim,
in fratricidal battles we reduce each other's claims too far
by blood, land lies desolate, as warriors make their name.

Kiwi Tamaki died near Scenic Drive, death's turn pointing,
first age came to a close, white sails appear, foreboding.

Tau Iwi

Came new turehu, but iwi not deceived, perceiving
men like them, old spirit, spirit of war in every race.
Yet the true anointed in the forest, still breathing,
matched the curious iwi heart, trees the sign of grace.

Internecine war, simple ills, and iwi too reduced
to resist tides of change, world changing, paradise too.
Trees fell, the climax forest breathed its last, it seemed,
though a seed for the future was planted by a few.

Metal crushes stone, yet rusts away, finite technology,
the hungry heart desires return to life, to love
of what was lost, crushed, spirit extinguished lightly,
so we became avatars, mimics of a lost life.

Can hope become reality, breathed by a true anointing
from the great Kaitiaki, we take up our caretaking.

Time to come

Our world will be, hills of green that run down to the sea
once more pillars from earth uphold the skyward vault
and we as avatars unmade, real people, real harmony
with all ourselves and all creation, no more in default.

The empty glass will soon enough be full of life,
as we devote to world renewing, home longed for
guarding what is precious, one people act as midwife
bring to birth once more, the great forest of Tiriwa.

We will walk among trees that call the holy name
of the one who breathed them life and power here
and our own names might be whispered there, a flame
of love and grace and power, to those who really care.

Avatars cross over in something not their natural state
we are life, nature redeemed, unless too long we wait.

March 25, 2010.

LIES AND DAMNED LIES

As Twain via Disraeli averred,
and as I have modernly concurred,
there are lies, and there is self-deception,
there are damned lies, and there is mass deception,
then there are statistics, but worst of all,
the specious science that employs them all.

December 20, 2014.

LAMENT FOR MICHELANGELO . . .

AND ALL GREAT ARTISTS.

Oh, we pity those who bring to mind, heart and spirit
The longing for the infinite, for God and his Christ
By means of rock, canvas, ink portray the ineffable
Cry out of the depths, our need of salvation unequivocal.

Shielded from healing, deliverance and salvation
By prodigious talent, in marble, paint and pen
Can a camel go through the eye of a needle?
Can one triple-blessed by God resist his call?

Your life sculpt, paint and write, with hammer and nail,
With blood and water portray, offer the great Hallel
Will you, with all God's gifting, squander life alone?
Will he not welcome you and all you love,
to an eternal home?

March 26, 2022, after reading his sonnets.

WORDS ARE . . .

Words are tumbling images
they fall like water falls,
turbulent and rough as rapids run
they shape, erode, smooth form
my mind, into bright marble halls
of statuary and colonnaded pillars,
all to be destroyed and then rebuilt
by that singular word,
God's truth and Spirit.

**During morning prayer time while reading Francis Schaeffer and the Bible,
February 17, 2017.**

THE CUP SAGA

Some mug has got those cups
For them there'll be no ups
It's down they go in Lynda's books
No saving for their pretty looks.
Let loose we say the hounds of hell
For them doth toll the requiem bell.

So be a true professional:
Return those cups and all is well.

School, August 20, 2013.

POETRY

Imagination, intellect, emotion
fused in the unity of Spirit
eliciting ungodly commotion
no one really wants to know it.

When the heart touches our minds
One must overthrow the other,
if either the creation spark burns
both want quickly to subdue it.

We self-limit to be one or the other,
cannot see our need for integration.
Thinker, feeler, and in all creator,
Of one purpose, holy regeneration.

The holy poets saw
and prophesied to all,
The word of God is more,
raising body and soul.

Be one, as I and the Father are One!

—John 17:11, 21–22

Wednesday, September 8, 2021. Inspired while reading John Stuart Mill and others on poetry. Their vision is too limited. Effective poetry, that is, poetry which effects a good response, integrates heart, mind and imagination, illumined with a flash of the Spirit, i.e., God's Holy Spirit enlightening our human spirit. It opens the door to revelation. This process may be negative, leading to hell, as well as positive, leading to eternal life. It is hellish when the inspiration is hellish, and the broad road to hell begins when we place our own spirit at the center. We must look beyond ourselves.

BIRTHDAYS AND LIFE

We never can prepare
though uneasily aware
of thirtieth, fortieth, sixtieth
(at eighty we don't care).
With the spirit of our youth
eyes preternaturally clear
we see the world as old
but our souls are ever new.

January 31, 2015.

ENCOURAGEMENT

Encouragement can seem so far away
When all we want is things to just remain
Life and joy when put in place to stay
Yet life just offers us a sad refrain.

But hope can spring from most unlikely places
Our strength and purpose still resolved to win.
We grasp the challenge, set our faces
And find the power and victory within.

June 24, 2009.

TEACHING ROCKS

Does teaching rock or am I teaching rocks?
that's the question, Mr. Principal.
If teaching rulz, are we teaching fools?
that's another problem, Boss.

And if teachers rock and rule,
inanimate objects and fools,
what does the head teacher do?

I'll tell you what the headmaster does, really,
he's not just another rock in the wall,
he's the cornerstone that keeps it all . . .
straight up!

He's the main man who makes the rules,
(and bends them as he pleases) . . . really.
but if he has a rock to rule his life,
his guiding star shines truly!

Yet other rocks support this wall,
they support it from below,
so it still stands tall, though the wind does blow
. . . and blow . . . and blow . . . and blow.

Now walls have a bad press, it's true,
they can separate and cause heartache, but . . .
the wall is rock that keeps harm out,
and rules can keep the goodness in.

The rocks and rules provide a home,
and the wall can keep the roof on,
a haven for our wandering stars,
our little high school rockers.

So, teacher man, hear what I say,
you built some walls and a covering too,
we wish you well,
but you *will* teach foreva.

May the kindly rocks and rules you built,
last another day,
may our next head rocker
on your foundation stay.

Rock on Boss, you can relax some of those old rules now!
or not?

June, 2006.

CREATION—REDEMPTION—SALVATION

Say what you think, my brother,
is man in evolution
or is it too much bother
to think of revolution
against the pile of bony facts
which show but adaptation
to think that man is not intact
but in a devolution.
And where did the downward spiral spring
but from the cradle of Eden
since when we've not improved a thing
save the spirit of rebellion.

Now rebels have an air of glory
to our self-satisfaction
yet up on heaven's seventh story
the odour of putrefaction.

So realise, man, that you're alive
God's holy act of creation
given to do and grow and thrive
an act of pure redemption.

If the redeemer sets our destiny
not look behind confusion
our faces turn against history
toward God's great solution.

The cross dissolves our sin and pain
life grows from resurrection,
so turn your face toward the Son
the only true salvation.

Good Friday, March 28, 1997.

PAIN IS A PAIN

Pain makes you go ouch!
it turns you into a bit of a grouch.
Why does God allow it?
well, I wouldn't mind just a little bit,
but pain makes you go ouch!

They say pain teaches you a lesson
but they don't know with whom they're messin'
I'll resist it and fight it
though I'll probably learn a little bit
cause pain does teach me a lesson!

Pain seems to last forever
sometimes oblivion is what we'd prefer
we drink and take drugs
so high that our eyes look like bugs
'cos pain seems to last forever!

Pain is mostly soon forgot
when I'm clear I just don't care a jot.
I feel sympathy for others
and try to help my unfortunate brothers
but pain is mostly soon forgot.

Pain is one hell of a question
it fiercely queries our spiritual position.
Do we trust a higher power
or would we rather take a cold shower?
'cos pain is one hell of a question!

September 8, 2015. in bed with a painful back for company.

Wordless Poems

Quiet certainty in a raging storm,
The blossom stays on the tree.

Thought can pierce steel as water destroys rock;
the wise man knows to wait.

A fragrant water lily covers the surface of a pond,
hiding depth.

The wind does not listen to the tree,
but the tree makes the wind known.

Everyone has a mind, but a mind that sings
is a great treasure.

Love, the greatest treasure on earth;
hold it gently in your palm.

In hard ground a flower struggles forth;
infinitely greater beauty.

Stranger in a strange land,
yet grace and beauty are always most welcome.

A mountain supports many forms of life,
sheltering the lowliest shrub.

Minds can cut and heal, like blades;
there is a time for each operation.

A man breaking stones in a quarry;
is he a builder or a convict?

A helping heart learns joy and sorrow;
the important thing is learning.

Hares do not race turtles but wolves;
to grow, always test yourself with equals.

Wind blows now gentle now powerful;
your mind bends or breaks fate appropriately.

Tree roots break apart concrete;
your will can shape your destiny;
perseverance.

No one gives a volcano permission;
lava flows, unstoppable.

Wisdom grows organically,
yet mind has an inorganic chemistry.

Nature takes risks with us;
dare to overcome and grasp the nettle;
courage.

Rock broken down by tree roots
becomes the tree;
victory.

Life overcomes the dark;
to the last breath,
Determination and wisdom.

No uncertainty in a charging bull;
be prepared to adapt.

Rivers meet and flow together;
many others add to their power;
friends.

Integrity does not depend on others,
but trust your close friends.

The heart of a tree is softer than bark,
but each one needs the other.

Enough heat melts steel;
a man's heart should always be malleable metal.

Gentle words can break bones;
the power of a peaceful spirit achieves much.

Good humor;
wisdom that teaches the ignorant;
bad humor pleases them.

Trees make music with the wind;
music plays us to please God and angels.

Veiled, waiting for the moment,
the warmth of spring reveals a lotus
though ice covered the pond.

Load-bearing, shade-giving branches
An oak tree, seen through swirling mist,
full strength not yet seen.

Bright fingers of dawn cascade
arms raised shine with golden light
the power of a pure heart.

Molten lava, lake of fire
enough spring rain cools the surface
power contained briefly.

Snowflakes, the beauty of symmetry
an indomitable yet yielding will
water is hard to grasp.

Swirling leaves playfully eddy
Autumn wind shakes vibrant colors
then peace, all is still.

Rich color, yellows and red
peace of mind in a raging world
finding the complete image.

Hidden strength is best
the way forward is soon found
as winter turns to spring.

A massive tree shelters birds
life a gift to both weak and strong
and power comes from within.

Life's vision in a teardrop
trust in the Lord, trust also in yourself;
melted ice becomes a mighty river.

Long summer days pass us by
finding our vision through the haze
suddenly we see clearly.

Energy and life break through,
flower and oak tree in the same soil;
gardens show strength and beauty.

Butterflies perish in the snow
only the brave and resolute run on ice;
swim strongly in life's current

Blue skies and a strong breeze,
a summer bird hovers overhead, singing;
the battle ground is prepared.

Water lilies bloom, radiant
the water of the pond deep and still;
twice as beautiful.

The way lies straight ahead
Yellow daffodils a field of promise
augur of a golden future.

Ice melts, spring water flows
though the warrior's way is hard
victory is to the brave.

Roses shine through a hedge
a bubbling brook joins a mighty river
life and joy overflow.

White rose on a stone wall
gentle power breaks the rock apart
a warrior princess stands forth.

Deep blue sky, shining stars
a gentle soul illuminates the world
light in the darkness.

A leaf blows across the landscape
a dance in time with all nature;
perfect!

Spring rains in the desert
Carpeted with flowers
One stands tall, roots supporting many.

A volcano lies sleeping—
Sudden explosion,
Beautiful fireworks.

A bull passes peacefully through the river
Then he attacks—
stay focused!

A tui lights on harakeke flowers,
so much nectar,
blessing flows.

Stone by stone was Jerusalem cast down,
stone by stone rebuilt,
our lives.

A field of roses summons,
a thornless summer of content,
and the muse.

The promise, Life,
uncompromising, unyielding,
always fulfilled.

Between the spaces of the universe
flows heart desire
the nightingale sings.

Green as dark green tea
Pools of fiery liquid jealousy
The curse of man.

Perfect reflection
strong wind ripples the water
the stone skips each wave.

Board in the white water
perfect tube and perfect ride
still wanting more.

Sunrise glow reveals
red flowers on a field of glory
peace is from the heart.

Stones across the land
treasure to the eye that sees
when cut, a diamond.

Antelope at a stream
a lion stalks, sudden attack
she easily skips away.

Red rose, morning dew
Desiccating wind blows strongly
Only one petal falls.

Tigers hunting as one
The forest hears no approach
The prey is assured.

A hawk circles high above
An eye that sees everything
Protecting the young.

A flight of doves circles
The wind blows good to us all
clouds form and reform.

Strong wind shakes the branch
cherry blossoms fall to earth
but we love cherries.

Wind and fire, water, earth
Trouble disturbs the unwary
But the saints know peace.

Mystery and nature
the clear space in the painting
full of meaning.

Sun and moon, heart and head
I don't know where they might lead
yet as above, below.

My words are not heard by many,
for better or for worse,
yet reside forever,
in the fabric of the universe.

Most written for departing Year 13 form-class students, 1997–2014; some for departing teachers.

Other Sonnets

THIRTY-SIX YEARS

Well met in a world of conflict, disparate
drawn to and yet conflicted, each other held
complementary, drawn by an unknown fate
yet inspired by his Spirit we were meld.

Life of adventure we have shared, hardly
daring to trust that we could prevail, daring
the tides of love and grace to come in, fully
walking so far together, seeking, hoping.

Short time it seems, these thirty-six gone by
and now our hearts are merging into one
as we know him and he knows us we fly
into that perfect rest where love is won.

I love you my sweet Sue, and have no doubt
from this hard world the Lord soon lifts us out.

2010

THE GRAMMAR OF LOVE—A LAMENT

*GOD'S UNREQUITED LOVE FOR US AND OURS FOR EACH
OTHER*

Love requires bold subject and bold object;
To indeterminate longing it never yields.
That we so often fail to attain it
Is well explained by all our human shields.

Lovers in their hearts think they're set free
By compelling passion and desire so felt.
Yet soon beyond what Eros hopes to see
Bright reason clouds the drive to be complete.

Armed forces muster quick to quell the flame
Custom, culture, age, they fence it in;
And right though reason seems, yet all the same
We know the bounds should be broke more often.

So, the love of God is rejected for safe thought
And many a lover's love has come to naught.

December 4, 2013.

THE GRAMMAR OF LOVE—A CELEBRATION

GOD'S LOVE FOR US FULFILLED AND OURS FOR EACH OTHER.

Love me, loved me, deeply now, forevermore
seeking you I sometimes lost my passion
a wonder that I ever came so sure
cluttered by my foolish inhibition.

Freedom! I am set free to love you true
heart cleansed, soul released to feel your heart
beat with mine eternally, as one not two
on your breast I lay, never to be apart.

The flame of love burns laser-like through strife
differences consumed in its ring of fire;
old reason subsumed embraces love in life
no limits now until our life expire.

May every lover's love stay all ablaze
and all of us accept God's loving gaze.

New Year's Eve, at midnight, 2014.

Songs for the Children of God

JERUSALEM—PSALM 122

Rejoice with those who say to you
We will go to the house of the Lord
Our feet are standing in your gates
O Jerusalem.

Chorus
O my brother and my friend
Peace be within you
House of the Lord our God
We will seek your good.

Jerusalem is close compact
as a city closely bound.
There the tribes of the Lord ascend
to praise his holy name.

Chorus

There the thrones for judgment stand
the thrones of David's house.
There the tribes of the Lord ascend
in accord with Israel's Law.

Chorus

Pray for the peace of Jerusalem
May those who love her be secure.
May there be peace within her walls
may there be rest in her towers.

Chorus

March, 1992.

MARANATHA

Holy, you are holy,
Loving, you are lovely,
Glorious, in your glory,
Jesus, I come to you.

Precious, blood of Jesus,
Mighty Son, of the Father,
Wounded, for our healing,
Jesus, we come to you.

Spirit, of the living God,
Two-edged sword, of revelation,
Given for our revival,
Spirit, please come to us.

Father, of the universe,
Lord, of the life in us,
Author, of salvation,
Father, please send your Son.

Jesus, we need you here now,
Lord, our need is desperate,
Lord, our only hope is you,
Jesus, please come to us.

Holy, you are holy,
Loving, you are lovely,
Glorious, in your glory,
Jesus, please come to us,
Jesus, please come to us,
Jesus, please come to us.
Maranatha, Lord Jesus, come soon.

December 27, 1991.

HOLY IS THE LORD: A CHILDREN'S ROUND

Holy is the Lord,
Faithful and true,
Holy, holy, holy.

Holy is the Lord,
Righteous and good,
Holy, holy, holy.

Holy is the Lord,
Faithful and true,
Holy is the Lord,
Righteous and good,
Holy, holy, holy.

Holy is the Lord,
Merciful and kind,
Holy, holy, holy.

Holy is the Lord,
Faithful and true,
Holy is the Lord ,
Righteous and good,
Holy is the Lord,
Merciful and kind,
Holy, holy, holy.

And so on. Encourage children to call out their own pairs of qualities and include them as you go along, e.g., glorious and strong, loving and meek, patient and gentle etc. A lesson on the nature of God could follow, explaining each of the qualities of God and relating them to the children's situation.

1991

GREAT AND HOLY ARE YOU LORD

Great are you Lord,
Great and worthy of all praise,
Great are you Lord,
Great and holy is your name.

And we will lift your name,
Yes we will lift your name,
high above every other name,
And we will sing your praise,
for all eternity,
Yes we will sing your praise,
for you are holy.

Holy, are you Lord,
Holy, in clouded mystery.
Holy, are you Lord,
But you have touched our history.

And we are changed like you,
Yes we become like you,
seated on the throne with you,
Though we cast down our crowns,
for all eternity,
Yes we cast down our crowns,
for you are holy.

Great are you Lord!

January 2, 1991.

KING AND LORD: THE COMMITMENT SONG

My heart will sing a song of praise,
my voice will raise,
my voice will raise your holy name on high.

Chorus
Holy, holy, Lord Jesus Savior,
Holy, holy, Messiah King,
Holy, holy, one God almighty,
Holy, you are my everything.

Everything I give to you, all I am,
all I have belongs to you, my Lord,
Form me, use me as you will, in love,
I'll bear the cross with you this day, my King.

Chorus

All I am and all I do is thru your grace,
all my life I'll follow you, my Lord.
Consume me in the fire of love, by faith,
I'll drink the cup with you this day, my King.

Chorus

Anointed one, Messiah-Christ, you are our friend,
filled with grace and power and life, our Lord.
Dipped us in the Lamb's pure blood, set free,
for life in service to you now, our King.
Holy, holy . . .

(Men and women in unison: women = coda; men = chorus.)
***Coda*: Our hearts will sing a song of praise,**

our voice will raise,
our voice will raise your holy name on high.
Chorus: Holy, holy, Lord Jesus Savior,
Holy, holy, Messiah King,
Holy, holy, One God almighty,
Together: Holy, you are our everything,
Holy, you are our mighty King,
Holy, you are our God.

1990

Good News,
an Epilogue

GOOD NEWS

Good news, bad news, nearly numbed by it all,
tender conscience of my youth scarce can recall.
Yet though my sensitivity be dulled, quite uncouth,
memory still holds the shocks of my frailty,
of being right and being wrong,
found out by harsh reality.

I know I cannot be entirely right,
he who whispers in my ear, graceless wight,
they lead me down the garden path to hell,
and though in grief and tears I do resist,
still may hear the sound of heaven's bell,
yet no power to desist.

I must confess, my burden is too great,
this putrid sack of bones weighs on my heart,
(as the tinker's son would have called our load).
All I do to ease the pain just another goad
and every struggle and every curse
tightens its hold on me.

But look, light breaks through, I may not trip.
Someone stronger than me can break that grip,
the death grip that I know is mortal sin,
vile habits which drive the nails firmly in.
real Christ, real world and my own heart,
drive me to conviction.

Embedded deep within my soul, I know,
old pain has taught that tortured lesson well.
If no hero comes to save me, somehow,
hopeless, I have doomed myself to hell.

Once more the light breaks through, I see the hand
nail-scarred, reach down to offer me salvation.
Strengthened bodily, graced with a mind renewed,
I rise and stand in humble gratitude.
He suffered my pains and died in my place,
for me alone and for every lonely sinner.

Somehow, I realise, he is the one,
who only has the power to overcome.
A grace none else can offer,
none other could so suffer.
None else could step down from that glorious throne,
meet us where we are, so far from our true home.
And so, my lips break out in everlasting praise,
to Jesus my great Savior,
now and until, those great and glorious days.

Good news it was indeed that healed my troubled soul,
one day that saving grace, will make my body whole.
The bad news of the world now has no grip on me,
no second death but life in full, for eternity.

June 2, 2023.

Glossary

Anacreon—A Greek lyric poet, 582–485BC, notable for his drinking songs and hymns, here typifying the worldly person.

antipodes—Points opposite each other on a line drawn through the center of the earth, so New Zealand is typically called the Antipodes with respect to Britain, although more exactly it is the antipode of Spain.

archon—Based on a Greek word meaning *ruler*, here a glorious heavenly creation of God, the church.

Armageddon—The place of the final battle in this age between the forces of light (the good angels and redeemed humans with Christ as their leader) and the forces of darkness (demons and the God-rejecting *earth-dwellers* with Antichrist as their leader). The literal location includes Carmel and the plain of Jezreel.

assize/great assize—Christ's final judgment of all—saints and sinners—literally after the period of his millennial rule, just preceding the creation of the new heaven and new earth and the descent of the New Jerusalem, our eternal home.

Babylon—Name of the ancient city of the Babylonian empire in the second millennium BC. Referred to as a type of the sinful world and in reference to the future, eschatological global system of cultural, religious and economic control instituted by the Antichrist and False Prophet.

catatonia—A state where a person, though seemingly awake, does not respond to external stimuli, often in reaction to extreme trauma.

Chateau d'If—An island fortress used as a prison, offshore from Marseille. Dumas used it in his novel, *The Count of Monte Cristo*. Elements of the story have parallels with the death and resurrection of Christ and our redemption.

Cherubim—The plural Hebrew form of the highest class of angel (cherubs) who among other things, guard the way to the Tree of Life and prevent mankind from returning to Eden. Satan was a cherub before being cast down for his prideful rebellion against God.

corporatization—A form of church management based on a business (corporate) model. Often criticized, rightly or wrongly, in some mega-churches for taking the focus away from various biblical aspects of church life.

de facto—Something existing in reality though not necessarily legitimised by law or statute. Here a reference to an interpretation of the Bible based mainly on its functional6ity, which has obvious dangers.

de fide—Of or by faith.

de jure—Literally 'by law' or 'by right.' It is applied to an interpretation of the Bible based in its pure authority as God's special revelation.

de profundis—'Out of the depths.' A reference to Ps 130 which describes a deep personal struggle and waiting on God.

distantiation—The process of becoming aloof from something, or losing faith in it. A problem often faced by theological students overwhelmed by the sheer volume of critical views they might encounter which undermine their personal beliefs. In biblical study becoming aware of the 'otherness' of the Bible with respect to how we see the world.

eschaton/eschatology—From the Greek word *eschatos* meaning 'last' or 'end.' Refers to the events of the very last days, the end times, or their study.

functional authority—A view of the authority of Scripture which is non-propositional, that even though the Bible has errors it is still functionally useful. This is opposed by propositional views of inerrancy that see the Bible as true.

gravitas—An ancient Roman virtue of high seriousness and weighty demeanour.

Hanukkah—Jewish festival of lights commemorating the events of the Maccabean revolt, celebrated around, and sometimes at, Christmas time.

harakeke—Māori term for the flax plant.

hermeneutic(s)—The interpretation of the Bible. Depending on the text we may take different modes of interpretation, for example literal compared to allegorical or symbolic.

higher criticism—Also called the *historical critical method*, focused on document sources for Bible texts and has a secular viewpoint. Not to be confused with textual criticism which compares different manuscripts to work out the best possible text for translation.

historical scepticism—Doubt about whether some events in the Bible happened as they are recorded.

horizons—In hermeneutical discussion this refers to a worldview, a total way of viewing reality. Broadly, the world of the biblical text and the world of the reader confront each other. Merging of the horizons occurs when the interpreter successfully, that is faithfully, reintegrates everything they have learned. It should be a continuous process.

insular observer—The often-disproved notion that we can isolate ourselves successfully from the biblical text and its meaning and view it completely impartially and objectively.

Iwi—Māori term for tribe, below which are the hapu (sub-tribe) and whanau (extended family).

Kaitiaki—Māori term for a guardian, protector, or conservator.

Kiwi Tamaki—A Waiohua paramount chief who lived in the eighteenth century whose seat of power was Maungakiekie (One Tree Hill) in Tamaki Makaurau (Auckland). He was defeated and killed in a battle in the southern Waitākeres by Ngāti Whātua warriors.

Mammon—Money or the material wealth of this world.

Messiah—The Jewish word for *The Anointed One* who would be the saviour or liberator of the Jewish people. Christ is simply Greek for anointed one so sometimes is written Jesus the Christ.

miasma—A noxious or poisonous atmosphere associated with swamps which was thought in the Middle Ages to carry the Black Death.

millennium—A thousand years. Refers in last-days scriptures to an apparently literal thousand years of Christ's rule after Armageddon.

Moebius/möbius/mobius—In mathematics a moebius strip is a surface which can be drawn on both sides without the pen leaving the paper, a non-orientable surface. Here it indicates something constantly recurring which cannot be understood from only one angle of perception.

perdition—An old word indicating the loss of the soul in hell, and eternal damnation.

Pesach (pron. Pay'sark)—The Jewish festival of Passover beginning on the fifteenth day of Nisan.

plenipotentiary—Invested with the full powers of the ruler or potentate who commissions them.

propositional content—The content of the Bible which has substance and form that can be studied objectively not just as an end in itself but as a means of knowing God and Christ.

remnant—Those who remain. A term used frequently in the Bible of people who are left after a judgment process. Mostly used to describe the few holy people who remain in difficult times and whom God has saved for himself, but sometimes to describe an unholy group.

Scenic Drive—The main road that runs roughly north-south through the Waitākere ranges.

Scientology—The technoreligion founded by L. Ron Hubbard in 1954, based on practices called *dianetics*.

self-authentication—The inspiration of Scripture is evident in its self-authentication, with direct claims to divine inspiration within Scripture and the evidence of its prophecies and histories verified.

Shalom—Hebrew word for peace, harmony, prosperity, and wholeness.

stigmatic—The stigmata are the marks of the crucifixion on Christ's body. A saint who manifests these is referred to as a stigmatic or stigmatist.

super-reader—A term to describe a theoretical but non-existent person whose understanding of every aspect of biblical interpretation is so sound we can just take their word for it.

Tau Iwi—A Māori term for people who arrived in New Zealand well after Māori had settled in the land.

Tiriwa—The Māori name for the Waitākere forest, and the name of the leader of the Turehu tribe the first Māori settlers the Tainui encountered after they landed in New Zealand. The Turehu were not entirely human, having come from the earth, and they were probably thought of by Māori in the same way Europeans think of elves, like the elves of *Lord of the Rings*, not the pixie variety. Tiriwa had miraculous powers and could be seen as a type of spiritual archon or guardian angel who handed authority over the land to the Māori people who had arrived. Later, when the gospel arrived, many Māori recognised that authority was through Christ, who was Lord of all creation.

Turehu—See Tiriwa.

Waitākere—A low mountain range of regenerating climax forest of kauri and podocarps along the western coast of Auckland, on the remnant rim of a vast ancient volcano. The name means deep water (wai, water; takue, deep).

weal—Used as a synonym of *welt* (Anglo Saxon) to indicate the number of blows and injuries we might suffer in life (unlike the Old/Middle English synonym for *wealth*).

Zen Buddhist—Zen is a Japanese form of contemplative Buddhism derived from Indian (Dhyana) and Chinese (Chan) traditions.